Bible Study

7 SESSIONS FOR SMALL GROUP
AND PERSONAL USE

I Ams

Who Is Jesus?

Copyright © Waverley Abbey Trust 2023.

Published 2005 by Waverley Abbey Trust, Waverley Abbey House, Waverley Lane, Farnham, Surrey GU9 8EP, UK. Registered Charity No. 294387. Registered Limited Company No. 1990308.

The right of Christine Leonard to be identified as the author of this work has been asserted by her in accordance with the Copyright, Designs and Patents Act 1988, sections 77 and 78.

All rights reserved. No part of this publication may be reproduced, stored in a retrieval system, or transmitted, in any form or by any means, electronic, mechanical, photocopying, recording or otherwise, without the prior permission in writing of Waverley Abbey Trust.

For list of National Distributors, visit waverleyabbeytrust.org/distributors

Unless otherwise indicated, all Scripture references are from the Holy Bible, New International Version® Anglicised, NIV® Copyright © 1979, 1984, 2011 by Biblica, Inc.® Used by permission. All rights reserved worldwide.

Other Bible translations

Scripture quotations are from The ESV® Bible (The Holy Bible, English Standard Version®). Copyright © 2001 by Crossway, a publishing ministry of Good News Publishers. Used by permission. All rights reserved. Scripture taken from *The Message*. Copyright © 1993, 1994, 1995, 1996, 2000, 2001, 2002. Used by permission of NavPress Publishing Group. Scripture taken from the New King James Version®. Copyright © 1982 by Thomas Nelson. Used by permission. All rights reserved.

Front cover image: Adobe.

Concept development, editing, design and production by Waverley Abbey Trust

Printed in the UK.

Paperback ISBN: 978-1-78951-499-5

Ebook ISBN: 978-1-78951-500-8

Contents

- 4   INTRODUCTION TO THE COVER TO COVER SERIES
- 6   ABOUT THE AUTHOR
- 7   INTRODUCTION
- 11   **WEEK ONE**
  His Name is… 'I AM'
- 17   **WEEK TWO**
  'I AM the Bread of Life'
- 23   **WEEK THREE**
  'I AM the Light of the World'
- 29   **WEEK FOUR**
  'I AM the Good Shepherd and Gate for the Sheep'
- 35   **WEEK FIVE**
  'I AM the Resurrection and the Life'
- 41   **WEEK SIX**
  'I AM the Way, the Truth and the Life'
- 47   **WEEK SEVEN**
  'I AM the Vine; You are the Branches'
- 53   LEADER'S NOTES
- 67   DAILY GUIDE

About Cover to Cover

The *Cover to Cover* Bible Study Guides are a popular series helping individuals and groups to engage with the Bible and to dig deeper.

The first studies were produced in 2002 by Selwyn Hughes and now cover more than 80 different themes, characters and books of the Bible, and are compiled by various writers and Bible teachers.

How to Get the Best from the Studies

The *Cover to Cover* studies are designed to be either worked through individually or in a group. Whichever way you are using the study we encourage you to begin with prayer, asking God through His Holy Spirit to work in your life through these studies. Then trust that He will!

Do allow enough time for the questions and exercises, not rushing through but allocating time to focus on questions that raise specific challenges.

If you are studying as a group you may find our online resources useful. Here you will find some extra video content and copies of the daily guide to distribute to the members. Visit **wvly.org/c2ccv** to discover what is available.

In group discussions do make use of the leader's notes at the end of the study. Ensure that you give everyone in the group time to share and avoid allowing one person to dominate conversation.

Please feel free to adapt the material according to your group's needs. Trust that God is with you, leading you and helping each one of you draw closer to Him.

About the Author

Written by Chris Leonard

Chris Leonard leads many creative writing workshops and holidays and, with a degree in English and theology, she has 21 books published. Chris and her husband live in Surrey, England, have two grown-up children and three young grandchildren. She can be contacted at **chrisleonardwriting.uk**.

Introduction

Who is Jesus? What does that mean for us? These two very simple yet amazingly profound questions are at the heart of Christians' lives and faith – and also central to the message of John's Gospel. Written later than the others, it differs from Matthew, Mark and Luke's more straightforward accounts of Jesus' life. John, as perhaps the disciple closest to Jesus, (see John 21:20–25) reveals more of His inner thoughts and heart. John's rich picture-language uses familiar objects to explore multi-layered truths about who Jesus is. His Gospel also calls to mind countless references from the Jewish scriptures (our Old Testament).

Whether you've known Jesus for decades or met Him only recently, John's Gospel has plenty to say to you! No one needs education, special knowledge or brainpower to know Jesus, nor to understand John's simple vocabulary. Yet you could study Jesus in this rich Gospel forever and still find fresh angles and layers to explore. In this booklet, we'll be concentrating on just a few and hardly touching on some of John's important themes. Our main topic is Jesus' seven 'I am' sayings, which are unique to John. To communicate different aspects of His identity, Jesus used picture-language: bread, light, shepherd, gate, way, truth, resurrection, life and vine. That's nine nouns, but 'I am the way, the truth and the life' is taken as one saying, making the perfect seven. The Hebrew word for 'seven' signifies completeness, wholeness and perfection – since, on the seventh day, God declared His creation good and complete.

The first C2C Bible Study on John's Gospel is by Dr John Hacking and considers the seven miraculous 'signs' that *show* who Jesus is. (Other Gospels use the word 'miracles'.) Sometimes a 'sign' leads to an 'I am' saying that *tells*, in picture-language, who He is – for example, Jesus feeding the 5,000 leads to 'I am the bread of life'. We are focusing on the seven 'I am sayings', which all appear in John's first 15 chapters. Chapters 16–22 are vital, too, so we won't ignore them entirely!

Let's return now to that central question of John's Gospel: 'Who, exactly, is Jesus?' Writers of Psalms and other scriptures often proclaim: 'The LORD is my... light, shepherd, way,' etc. Yet imagine if someone asked, 'Who are you?' and you replied: 'I am the light of the world!' They'd likely conclude you were mad, bad, or possibly dangerous! When Jesus said He was those things and when people talked about what they had seen Him being and doing, gradually it became clear that He was claiming to be God, whose sacred name *Yahweh* means, literally, 'I am that I am'. Furthermore, Jesus' 'I am' sayings in John always use the Greek words *ego* (meaning 'I') and *eimi* (meaning 'I am'). That construction sounds normal to English speakers. In Greek and other languages such as Spanish, however, only the word for 'am' is used, unless implying extreme emphasis – as in 'I myself really am!' (The only *ego eimi* not in the seven sayings occurs in John 18:5 and 8, as Jesus emphasises *He* is Jesus of Nazareth, deflecting the soldiers from pursuing His disciples.) To religious Jews, a person claiming to be *Yahweh* was blaspheming and Jesus faced their murderous opposition for appearing to break *Yahweh's* law in the worst possible way.

Other titles expressing Jesus' name and identity occur in John's Gospel – Son of God, Son of Man, Saviour, Messiah or Christ, for example – and John 1 begins by naming Jesus 'The Word'. We communicate with words. God sent His beloved Son, Jesus, to take on flesh so that He could express the Godhead's 'I am-ness' (or who God is) in a form we could begin to understand – and ultimately to save us for eternal life with

INTRODUCTION

Him. God's 'Word' might also speak of the Father's bond (or guarantee) that He loves and gives everything to save us.

Drawing only on certain passages within John's Gospel isn't ideal. You could begin by simply reading a few chapters a week in your group, letting God speak to you and noticing how Jesus' 'I am' sayings fit within the whole. As you read, look out for the way John addresses three questions about Jesus: 'Who corroborates or "witnesses" that Jesus is who He says He is?' 'Did He stay true to His proclaimed identity?' And 'How does all this affect His followers and others here on Earth?' Notice too where 'I am…' becomes 'Now you are…', whether expressed in John or elsewhere in the New Testament. 'You are the light of the world.' 'You feed and shepherd my sheep.' 'You're a branch of my vine; my life flows through you. Embody my way, my truth and rise with Me!'

When it comes to the weekly studies, don't necessarily read all the passages suggested. Concentrate on those in John. There won't be time within a session to discuss all the questions, so choose those most appropriate for your group. If you would welcome a different kind of material, perhaps devotional, to use alongside this book, I would recommend Malcolm Guite's sequence of eight short poems on Jesus' 'I am' sayings, from his book *Parable and Paradox* (Norwich: Canterbury Press, 2016), pages 55–62. As in John's Gospel, the language is simple, the theology sound, the meaning straightforward – yet they take me to fresh depths, breadths and heights.

WEEK ONE
His Name is... 'I AM'

Warm Up

Let everyone introduce themselves in one quick sentence, starting with 'I am', then their name and just one thing that identifies them: maybe their job, a role in their family, or a characteristic such as 'the noisy one' or 'the reliable one'.

Bible Readings

- John 8:48–58
- John 1:1–42

Opening Our Eyes

Who is God? In ancient times, name denoted character; for example, 'Jesus', a variant of 'Joshua', means 'Saviour'. God goes by several names in the Old Testament, most significantly *Elohim* (plural of *El*, meaning 'God'), first used in Genesis 1 when God creates everything. *El Shaddai* means 'Almighty God'; *Adonai* means 'my Lords' (again, plural). Astoundingly, it's exiled murderer Moses who learns the holiest name of all through a flaming bush in the remote Sinai desert (Exodus 3). 'I am that I am,' he is told. Hebrew has no tenses for its verbs, only a sense of whether an action is complete (finished) or ongoing, which means God's name could read: 'I will be what I will be'. Confusing for us, perhaps, but since God is eternal, past, present and future are all the same to Him.

Transliterated from Hebrew as *YHWH* or *Yahweh*, this name occurs 6,800 times in the Old Testament and is often written 'LORD' in English Bibles. By Jesus' time, *YHWH* was considered so holy that only the High Priest was allowed to pronounce it, once a year, at the Feast of Atonement. To most people in Israel this *YHWH* must have seemed remote and unknowable.

God's other Hebrew names ('Almighty' and 'LORD') show aspects of who He is. 'I am', though, carries infinite meanings, implying that God is eternal, with no beginning or end, all-powerful, always present, all-sufficient, answerable to no one, boundless... all coming from an ordinary verb that we use many times a day! In reply to 'Who are you?' I might say: 'I am Chris, a writer' – never simply, 'I am'. Yet, after being asked, 'Who do you think you are?' Jesus says, 'Before Abraham was born, I am!' (John 8:58). Jewish leaders, hearing Him apparently blaspheming *Yahweh's* sacred name, rush to stone Him. They never do accept Jesus' true identity and later will cause Him to be crucified. It's rare for Jesus to say who He is directly in Matthew, Mark or Luke, though He might hint through a story or ask: 'Who do you say that I am?' In John's Gospel, He identifies

HIS NAME IS... 'I AM'

Himself obliquely as 'Son of Man' twelve times, though never claims that 'I am' this mysterious figure directly. In John 8:48–58, He says what He's not, then speaks of 'my Father' (the One they claim is their God) 'who glorifies me.' Then, in His astounding words: 'Before Abraham was, I am!' (ESV). Jesus affirms that He is divine – and eternal.

John 1:1–14, known as John's 'Prologue', sums up the themes of his Gospel, including who, exactly, Jesus is and His relation to both Father God and humankind. People spend years exploring these 14 image-packed verses. Written in the third person, with many Scripture references, they contain no 'I ams' but identify Jesus most clearly as 'the Word' – the living communication-link between heaven and earth, time and eternity, God and people. As Hebrews 1:1–2 says: 'In the past God spoke to our ancestors through the prophets at many times and in various ways, but in these last days he has spoken to us by his Son'. In subsequent chapters, Jesus tells us who He is, notably through the seven 'I ams' – and shows us, too, through His seven 'signs'. To the early disciples, including John, we owe the good news of who the young man, Jesus of Nazareth, really was and how He can save us. Now it's our turn to spread that Gospel!

Notes

Discussion Starters

1. What do you learn about who God is and what He is like from Exodus 3 – especially from His name *Yahweh* or 'I am that I am'?

2. The one true God is known by several different names. Might the plural forms hint at the Trinity? How do you address our three-in-one God – and each Person of the Trinity? What do those names mean to you?

3. What effects do knowing God's name and nature as 'I am that I am' (eternally present) have on Moses, on your life and on the world around you?

4. What effect does knowing Jesus is also 'I am' (divine, eternal, complete, etc.) have? See John 8:48–58.

HIS NAME IS... 'I AM'

5. Focusing on Jesus' identity and relationship to His Father and to us, what do you learn from the following:
   a. (a) John 1:1 (the Prologue)
   b. (b) John 1:19 (what Jesus' cousin John the Baptist says about Him)
   c. (c) John 1:36 (Jesus meets His first followers and Nathanael makes an amazing declaration).

6. How many names or titles of Jesus can you find in John 1 as a whole, and have you learnt any more about Him from them today?

Personal Application

Study and discussion are great, but when John's two disciples, curious about Jesus, ask where He's staying, He says, simply: 'Come and see'. They spend the day with Him. Then Andrew brings his brother. Philip tells the questioning Nathanael to 'come and see' too. Having met Him, these men declare truths about who Jesus is and the word spreads. So... spend time with Jesus, then tell others what you've just discovered about Him. You'll have unique understanding and opportunities. For example, Glenda has advanced terminal motor neurone disease and can't walk or speak. When she chose the song 'Because He lives, I can face tomorrow', the congregation understood the daily difficulties she faces, yet her radiant face showed that those words hold true for her and that Jesus still lives, loves and empowers today!

Seeing Jesus in the Scriptures

When Jesus declared openly who He was, hostile reactions would follow. That's understandable. 'What, Joseph's son from obscure Nazareth being God on Earth, and our Saviour? Ludicrous. Blasphemous pride. A dangerous madman, He'll cause endless trouble.' So, Jesus revealed His true identity little by little and often through His actions – John calls some of them 'signs' – and picture-language, such as 'I am the bread of life'. As with parables in the other three Gospels, 'whoever has ears to hear' will understand, while those who are not yet ready won't be alienated from the outset. Jesus also relied, as He still does, on us, His followers, communicating who He is through our actions, attitudes and words.

WEEK TWO
'I AM the Bread of Life'

Warm Up

When all have gathered, take a bread roll; pray, blessing it, one another and your time together, then pass it around, each pulling off a piece to eat. Keep silence a moment, then each share what you sense through your six senses: touch, taste, smell, sight, sound and 'God-sense'.

Bible Readings

- John 6:13, 21
- Exodus 16

Opening Our Eyes

I've never known extended hunger, though once was caught out with friends a long way from any food. We could think of nothing else until we found some! God knows we need food to live. He tells us to feed the hungry and has even provided food directly sometimes, as when He supplied manna-bread to keep all Israel alive for 40 years in the Sinai desert. Or when God fed the prophet Elijah and a poor widow by renewing her bread-making ingredients daily (2 Kings 4).

An account of Jesus feeding vast crowds of hungry followers appears in all four Gospels but John's retelling never fails to astound me. Including both a 'sign' and an 'I am' saying, John 6 shows Jesus' compassionate longing to supply far more than our physical needs. Truths revealed through many layers of reference resonate right back through the Scriptures and forward to impact the way Jesus wants us to live today.

Jesus' miracles seemed to offer physical comfort and security to the poor and vulnerable of those days. So many followed Him, relentlessly, until Jesus startled them by declaring: 'I am the bread' (v35). Multiplying a picnic lunch to feed a hungry crowd is one thing – but imagine being in that crowd and hearing: 'This bread is my flesh, which I will give for the life of the world' (v51) and you are to eat it (v.54). How shocking! No wonder that many who had been His disciples abandoned Him at this point (vv66–70). If you read on into John 7, you'll see how Jesus' words continued to provoke opposition, danger and persecution. We're familiar with the role of bread and wine at Communion Services, but Jews, with their strong prohibitions against consuming any creature's blood, were outraged. Later, Gentiles accused Christians of cannibalism.

Before His resurrection, even Jesus' closest disciples had very limited understanding that He had to die, let alone the reasons why. Some had, though, begun to see that Jesus offered more

'I AM THE BREAD OF LIFE'

than material relief – that believing in Him, feeding on Him and His words, however strange that seemed, would lead them to eternal life. The other Gospel writers made the bread-flesh connection clear while writing of Jesus' final Passover meal (see Matt. 26:19–29; Mark 14:12–26; Luke 22:7–22). John, though, having established it in chapter 6, in chapter 13 concentrates on Jesus showing 'the full extent of His love' through humble service and willingness to give His life. Is it coincidence that John also emphasises that Jesus dips bread into a bowl and gives it to Judas, echoing Psalm 41:9: 'Even my close friend, someone I trusted, one who shared my bread, has turned against me'? What love, what sacrificial grace Jesus showed!

In John 21, having already supplied bread and cooked some fish for breakfast, Jesus told Peter to 'feed my sheep'. Peter, the trusted 'rock', had denied Him three times and failed to understand so much. Yet it was also Peter who declared that only Jesus had the words of eternal life and kept on following Him (John 6:68–69). Most Christians I know have a lot in common with Peter. Like him, we mess up sometimes. Like him, we have Jesus' words of eternal life, we feed on Him and He forgives, restores and trusts us, often to do greater things! So let's keep feeding on Him, the bread of life – and then showing others where to find that same bread!

Notes

Discussion Starters

1. 'Passover' and 'bread' link this week's passages. How has your spiritual understanding increased through reading about them?

2. The Romans kept their citizens happy with 'bread and circuses' (food and exciting entertainment). Jesus offers something very different. Do you follow Jesus mainly to satisfy your material needs, security, comfort or entertainment? How can we receive the joy and nourishment we need to follow Him more closely and live more fully?

3. Jesus taught His disciples to pray: 'Give us each day our daily bread' (Luke 11:3). How has Jesus being 'living bread' enlarged your understanding of this prayer?

4. Are you prepared for the cost, backlash, even possible danger involved in following Jesus? Are you prepared to shock sometimes, as well as to comfort?

'I AM THE BREAD OF LIFE'

5. When has trusting Jesus enabled you to be generous, even when it seemed you had little to give?

6. How does Jesus guide and empower us to help people in physical and spiritual need?

7. Why might John have emphasised the dipped bread Jesus gave to Judas?

8. If you've ever failed, betrayed or denied Jesus, what can you learn from 1 Corinthians 11:32 – and from Jesus' restoration of Peter in John 21?

Personal Application

God gave Israel manna enough for each day's needs: any excess hoarded would turn bad overnight (Exod. 16:17–20). Are you always wanting more, or content with 'enough', a hoarder, or able to rest in Jesus' generosity and be generous yourself? Jesus promised that we will never hunger again (John 6:35), yet Christians do still starve to death. He would have been almost dead Himself after 40 days fasting in the wilderness but trusted His Father, saying, 'Man shall not live on bread alone, but on every word that comes from the mouth of God' (Matt. 4:4), and, later, 'Blessed are those who hunger and thirst for righteousness, for they will be filled' (Matt. 5:6). Explore and pray through these paradoxes.

Seeing Jesus in the Scriptures

Read the last paragraph of 'Opening our Eyes' again. In John 21, Jesus suppled fish too, then told His disciples how to land 153 more. How odd to stop and count 153 wriggling fish tearing at their nets! The number may well be symbolic, since, apparently, the number of nations known at that time was 153, so many theologians see in John 21 a version of the Great Commission – 'go and make disciples of all nations… teaching them' (Matt. 28:19–20). Catching so many fish may be one example of Jesus turning an 'I am' into 'I've shown you and now am commissioning you to do what I do'. 'I am the bread of life and the good shepherd. Now you do the same. Call, then feed and disciple my sheep!' Or 'Go catch fish!'

WEEK THREE
'I AM the Light of the World'

Warm Up

Have you ever experienced total darkness? If you have, share your reactions and any problems you faced. If not, imagine yourselves living 2,000 years ago, with only dim rush lights or, if you were relatively well off, an oil lamp. What would light have meant to you?

Bible Readings

- John 9:1–41
- John 1:1–9
- John 12:34–46

Opening our Eyes

Good and evil, light and darkness are huge themes throughout the Bible, especially in John's letters and Gospel. His original readers would have known many Old Testament references to light and darkness – also, perhaps, Jesus' words about light recorded in Matthew, Mark and Luke, since John's Gospel was written after the other three. Light is a big factor in many other religions too but while they are 'dualistic', seeing light and darkness in a constant and equal struggle, the Bible proclaims God's light inextinguishable. Jesus is, supremely, that light. Despite wars, disasters, heresies and persecutions, the light He brought into this world as a tiny baby that first Christmas has spread worldwide and has never stopped shining. To us it feels sometimes as though evil is gaining the upper hand, but to rid a room of darkness, we don't scoop it up and pour it down the drain: we switch on a lamp or we light a candle, however feeble.

The start of John's Gospel parallels that of Genesis. Apart from bioluminescence, science shows that all life on earth is powered, directly or indirectly, by our sun. According to Genesis, though, God created light before the sun and other stars. Plants, then animals, followed. You don't have to believe in a literal seven-day creation to wonder if the writer of Genesis unknowingly prophesied the deeper truth expressed in Hebrews 1:3 (ESV) – that Christ is 'the radiance of the glory of God' and 'upholds the universe by the word of His power'. Jesus is and always was the powerhouse, setting the universe alight, sparking life from darkness and chaos. His Christmas birth heralded God's new (or renewed) creation that would be completed, finally, at Christ's second coming.

In the Old Testament, any who glimpsed God's holy and glorious light were overwhelmed or even died. Jesus came to Earth to reveal God's light and holiness in a way leading not to death but to our eternal life. How ironic, then, that the most religious of the very people God had chosen to be a 'light for

'I AM THE LIGHT OF THE WORLD'

the Gentiles' (Isa. 49:6 etc) had become 'foolish and senseless'. They had 'eyes that did not see', as Jeremiah 5:21 says. They wrote off the very people who did recognise Jesus' light (often the blind, sinful, unwell, poor, foreigners, children or women) as beyond salvation.

In John 9, the conversation between religious leaders and the man Jesus healed of blindness becomes almost comical. The 'ordinary' lay man is astonished that devout learned leaders can't see the good Jesus has done. His family's straightforwardly honest reactions and 'witness statements' also contrast with the leaders' distortion of God's truth. Those leaders, not the physically sightless man, refuse to accept the light, blinding themselves rather than letting the Saviour enlighten them. Jesus' response to them echoes Isaiah 5:20: 'Woe to those who call evil good and good evil, who put darkness for light and light for darkness, who put bitter for sweet and sweet for bitter.'

In the days before street lighting, those still travelling home as night fell might have found themselves truly 'in the dark' – lost and in danger. In John 12:46, Jesus says: 'I have come into the world as a light, so that no one who believes in me should stay in darkness.' In today's world of fake news, media 'influencers', 'cancel culture' and 'anything goes' values, how we need to stay in His light! Consider what light – whose light – do you see by?

Notes

Discussion Starters

1. John 1:1–9 starts like Genesis 1. What do their key words 'light', 'darkness', 'the world' and 'life' tell you about Jesus, 'Light of the World'?

2. 'The light shines in the darkness, and the darkness has not overcome (or understood) it' (John 1:5). What do you understand by that, and what difference does it make to the world?

3. 'While I am in the world, I am the light of the world' (John 9:5). What happens now Jesus isn't with us in the flesh?

4. 'In your light, we see light' (Psalm 36:9). In whose light do you see God, the world, other people and yourself?

'I AM THE LIGHT OF THE WORLD'

5. Where might you still be blind, resisting the true light? How can you remain walking in Jesus' light or return to it, having strayed (1 John 1:7)?

6. In John 9, some are blind to Jesus' light; others perceive it. In the culture you know, who is blind to Jesus' light, who sees it – and why?

7. What do our passages in John show of Jesus' light overcoming darkness? Where have you seen this happen?

8. Into which dark bits of the world are you shining God's light? See Matthew 5:14–16.

Personal Application

Jesus, *the* Light of the world said these astounding words to His disciples: '*You* are the light of the world' (Matthew 5:14–16). Does that mean we 'bear witness to the light', as John the Baptist did, telling others about Jesus and righteousness? Yes, but there's more. We are His light-bearers on Earth because He makes His life and His light available to us – He's put them in us. Do you believe that? If many failed to see the perfect light of the incarnate Son of God, now, when His light is filtered through our many imperfections, what hope is there? Yet, noticing how our ways, especially our love, differ from the norm, some will be intrigued and ask questions. May Jesus' light and love shine through our actions, attitudes – the whole way we live our lives – as well as through the truths we speak.

Seeing Jesus in the Scriptures

What does Jesus' light do, according to Scripture? He enlightens us about God and brings the light of hope, love and compassion to the poor, outcast and unclean, to those who mourn, are tormented, ill or disabled in some way. His light of freedom penetrates dungeons of sin, shame and guilt, illuminating the way to new relationships, purpose and fullness of life in God. Jesus kindles a new creation in us so that, walking in His light, we can continue His work on Earth. No one individual can shine light in all the ways He did – but where and how is He asking you to try?

WEEK FOUR
'I AM the Good Shepherd and Gate for the Sheep'

Warm Up

Think of all the biblical stories and references to sheep and shepherds you can in five minutes. Or, if the group and meeting place are up to it, ask one member to be 'shepherd' rounding up the remainder, cast as two-legged sheep. (NB This is an energetic but non-contact sport!)

Bible Readings

- John 10
- Ezekiel 34
- Matthew 7:13–14

Opening Our Eyes

John 10 offers three 'I ams' for the price of one! 'I am the good Shepherd' and 'I am the gate for the sheep' are joined by a third. Appearing in reported speech and in two slightly different forms, it is not included in John's seven 'I ams'. Did you spot it?

As a child, I read about 'the door of the sheep' and objected: 'Animals don't have doors in them!' So I'm relieved the NIVUK translates John 10:7 as 'the gate *for* the sheep'. In Jesus' time, sheep or shepherds would have been an everyday sight, but not now for most of us. Sheep husbandry has changed too! I've watched quadbike and dog rounding up sheep but the Hebrew word for 'shepherd' means 'sheep-feeder' – one who led, rather than herded, his sheep to pasture. Before nightfall, each shepherd led his flock to a communal sheepfold – a circular structure that housed multiple flocks. Its substantial stone walls had one narrow entrance and all the sheep had to enter through it. Then, one shepherd would sit or lie across it all night, protecting the sheep from attack by thieves or wolves. Come morning, each shepherd would call to the sheep in his care and they followed him gladly to pasture.

Many scriptures show God as the true shepherd-king of Israel – guiding, leading and protecting His people. Starting as a shepherd boy, protecting his family's sheep from wild animals, David wrote of the Lord as his shepherd in Psalm 23 and later became one of Israel's few good kings. Exiled murderer Moses too learnt lessons shepherding his father-in-law's flock in the desert before being entrusted with shepherding Israel out of Egypt. Yet power corrupts and even such godly men went badly wrong at times. History and the Bible teem with truly exploitative kings, priests and prophets who led people astray. Ezekiel 34 is excoriating on the subject, and it's so applicable today.

'I AM THE GOOD SHEPHERD AND GATE FOR THE SHEEP'

Jesus' kind of leadership works very differently from norms today, or in the past. The semi-nomadic 'sheep-feeders' of Jesus' day lived roughly, outside of settlements and were considered untrustworthy. Some would steal sheep. Yet the first people invited to meet the infant Jesus, other than His immediate family, were shepherds – and Jesus trusted His future disciples, including us, to feed and protect His flock. 'Pastor' means 'shepherd'. That privilege and responsibility has been both honoured and horribly abused through the centuries, which is why we need to pay close attention to how Jesus shepherded. His authority came from His Father. When on earth, Jesus said, 'The Son can do nothing by himself; he can do only what he sees the Father doing' (John 5:19). Now He Himself, not our assumed version of Him, is the door, or entrance for the sheep, our protector as well as feeder. Religious leaders, and all with pastoral responsibilities, need to be wary of 'shepherding' their flock in the wrong direction. Some assert their own harsh authority rather than calling on God's loving care. Pastors and flock, all owe primary allegiance to Jesus as head of the Church. Ultimately, we all follow Him, in fellowship with one another.

First, Jesus stands at our door and knocks (Rev. 3:20). If we need to invite Him in, He'll lead us to His fold's entrance, where He lays down His life to keep ours safe. He'll call us in and out of the fold, shepherding us to receive and to give according to His ways, not our own. It's worth noting that none of the above would work if not based on the implied 'I ams' in John 10:29–30.

Notes

Discussion Starters

1. How do you hear and recognise Jesus' voice, distinguishing it from other voices?

2. Christians have been persecuted horribly at times and Jesus never promised us an easy or pain-free existence. So, what is the 'fullness of life' Jesus promises in John 10:10? Is it for now or only after we die?

3. Have you ever been 'robbed' of what Jesus has for you?

4. Jesus lays down His life for the sheep (John 10:11–18). How vulnerable are you prepared to be, for Him and for those in your care?

'I AM THE GOOD SHEPHERD AND GATE FOR THE SHEEP'

5. What do you understand by: 'There shall be one flock and one shepherd' (v16)?

6. What do John 10 and Ezekiel 34 show you about good or bad leadership – especially 'shepherding' in the church?

7. Do you see Jesus as your doorway into God's presence and into all you do in daily life? Have you tried other doorways, religious or secular?

8. In John 10:29–30, what were the additional 'I ams' and their implications for Jesus' hearers at the time – and for anyone who reads this passage today?

Personal Application

Jesus wants us to become more like Him. As the Light of the world told His disciples: 'You are the light of the world', so 1 Peter 5:2 exhorts: 'Be shepherds of God's flock… under your care, watching over them'. Acts 20:28 says: 'Keep watch over yourselves and all the flock of which the Holy Spirit has made you overseers. Be shepherds of the church of God'. Jesus calls all of us – not just clergy, other 'professional Christians' or special evangelists – to seek lost sheep and shepherd them gently back to His fold. Are we ready to defend them against the spiritual or psychological enemies that will deceive or rob them? Are we prepared to be inconvenienced or even 'lay down our lives' for them? Jesus is the ultimate shepherd and protector, but He wants us involved in leading as well as following and in praying for those who lead – parents, teachers, influencers, youth leaders, pastors as well as politicians.

Seeing Jesus in the Scriptures

In the other Gospels, Jesus often hides the truth about exactly who He is within parables. This, together with His tendency to ask those He's healed to tell no one, is known as the 'Messianic secret'. Reticence about who He was delayed arrest until 'His time' had come and avoided alienating those not yet ready to hear (Matt. 13:10–17). Looking at John 10 and some previous passages we've highlighted so far, what lessons in communicating spiritual truth can we learn from the gradual way in which Jesus has been showing and telling who He is?

WEEK FIVE
'I AM the Resurrection and the Life'

Warm Up

Tell where you've seen resurrection power and life at work. Perhaps in nature — leaf-fall and renewal, or recovery of land after a fire or severe drought. Perhaps when someone or something seemingly beyond hope revived and flourished against all human expectation.

Bible Readings

- John 11
- John 12:20–34
- John 20 and 21 (optional)

Opening our Eyes

When a baby is born, we wonder at the miracle of new life. When someone dies, even after a long life, at the deepest level, somehow, it comes as a shock. How can all that person was just… end? Could our very human sense that it's all wrong arise because death was never in God's original plan? According to the picture-language of Genesis 2 and 3, He meant people to live with Him, eating from the 'tree of life', rather than that of the knowledge of good and evil. Death is portrayed as His merciful way of shortening the mess, pain and toil caused later by lives of sin and rebellion against Him.

In John 11, faced with His friend's death, Jesus was troubled and deeply moved. Yet much of His teaching in John 11 focuses less on the resurrection of Lazarus, who would die again, than on Jesus' own identity. Jesus always was and always will be 'the resurrection and the life'. Eternal God does not die. God built resurrection into creation itself, surely as day follows night and spring follows winter. Later, God's Son (the ultimate 'Life' and He who raised Lazarus) bore the deathly consequences of humanity's sins. How extraordinary that the ultimate 'Life' could actually die – for us! By giving up His sinless life, in obedience, Jesus glorified His Father. He overcame sin and its consequence; death and His glorious resurrection rejoins us to His life eternal. Paul wrote: 'If the Spirit of him who raised Jesus from the dead is living in you, he who raised Christ from the dead will also give life to your mortal bodies' (Romans 8:11). Think on that! Scripture says little about our lives after our bodies die. In John 3:3, though, Jesus famously tells Nicodemus that he must be born again. John's Gospel implies that our eternal life can start now – as a quality, rather than a quantity, of life that will transcend the decay of our earthly bodies and last beyond time itself. Look too at 1 Corinthians 15:19–21, where Christ is portrayed as not only the 'firstfruits' from the dead but also the new Adam (the name means 'man'). Human sin spoiled God's creation and brought death: by contrast, Christ inaugurated a new creation and continually brings life.

By John 11, Martha already recognised Jesus as Messiah and Son of God (v.27). That's controversial enough – but the raising of Lazarus happened at an extremely tense time politically. Several self-styled messiahs had been fuelling revolutionary feeling against the Roman occupiers of their land. Jewish leaders feared the people would rebel and the Romans crack down again, crucifying thousands and crushing all remaining Jewish authority. Just as most of the Jewish nation started converging on Jerusalem for Passover, news of Jesus' spectacular resurrection of Lazarus spread out of control. Jesus knew He risked excited multitudes proclaiming Him King of Israel as He entered Jerusalem and that Jewish leaders would redouble their efforts to eliminate Him. He also knew that, at Passover, 'His time' would come to restore our relationship with God. He Himself would act as the sacrificial Passover lamb, not once a year but for all time. Metaphorically, the 'angel of death' would 'pass over' those marked with Jesus' blood.

Who is Jesus? Jesus' death and subsequent resurrection proved Him, miraculously and uniquely, 'the resurrection and the life' as well as the humble, sacrificial Lamb of God and the true, righteous King – the only king who really will live and reign forever.

Notes

Discussion Starters

1. What do you learn from the way Martha, Mary, Thomas and Jesus reacted to Lazarus' death?

2. Jesus knew that raising Lazarus would fuel violence. How did He know it was 'His time'? Would you have taken such a risk?

3. Might your attitude to death and life shift as a result of this week's study?

4. What do you make of Jesus' radical words about glory in John 11 and 12?

'I AM THE RESURRECTION AND THE LIFE'

5. What is the eternal 'life in all its fullness' that Jesus promises those who trust in and follow Him? As He revives and restores what is dead or broken in us, how can we co-operate with Him?

6. How did Jesus treat His friends after His resurrection? How do you treat fellow Christians who are in emotional turmoil, who misunderstand, struggle to believe, or have let you or Jesus down?

7. 'Blessed are those who have not seen and yet have believed' (John 20:29). That's us! How do you 'bear witness' to Jesus being alive, demonstrating how He lives in you?

8. How is studying the passages this week helping you to 'believe that Jesus is the Messiah, the Son of God, and... [so] have life in his name' (John 20:31)?

Personal Application

Our times now, like those of Jesus' day, are becoming increasingly dark and troubled. Uncertainty, confusion, helplessness, isolation and fear seem all-pervasive. Stress, cynicism, anxiety, worry and depression build. Where is the 'fullness of life' Jesus promised? Does His resurrection bring us hope, or do we radiate gloom and despair? Have you come to know and trust Him as your source and anchor of love and goodness in a chaotic world? Do you live in the good of that, radiating faith in Him who leads us through dark valleys, who lights, guards, rescues, supplies our needs and satisfies our souls? If you're anything like me, not consistently. It's often in our dark, needy times that He remoulds us to become what He intended and to live as Jesus' distinctive 'Easter People'.

Seeing Jesus in the Scriptures

Jesus left the Father and Holy Spirit, giving up all heaven's privileges to live on Earth and then die for us in his early 30s. He never married, had children, wealth, or his own home. He made some friends and helped some people, within a limited area and time frame. He challenged bad attitudes and false thinking, taught godly wisdom and championed outcasts. He grew in grace and truth, did no wrong, but oh, how He suffered, laying down His life for the joy of saving and knowing us! Then His Father raised and glorified Him above all others. Is this fullness of life He offers 'simply' pure love – love that we're able to give inasmuch as we receive it from Him?

WEEK SIX
'I AM the Way, the Truth and the Life'

Warm Up

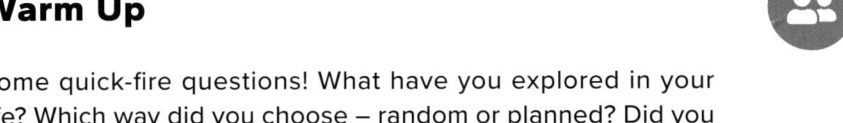

Some quick-fire questions! What have you explored in your life? Which way did you choose – random or planned? Did you follow the crowd, your own way, or a particular truth? What were the consequences if you took a wrong turning? What drew you back to God's way?

Bible Readings

- John 14
- Isaiah 30:9–21
- Isaiah 35:1–10 – The 'highway of holiness'
- Luke 10:25–37 – 'The good Samaritan'

Opening our Eyes

Early Christians became known as 'People of the Way' because they followed Jesus, the ultimate way, truth and life. Jesus' way and the truth of the cross are hard. They turn received truths and customary behaviour upside down, often leading to conflict, even to persecution and death.

As well as showing the truth by the way He lived, Jesus gave us clear, simple instructions. To paraphrase John 14: 'Know, believe, ask and love me. Do my works. Obey my commands and teaching. Receive the Spirit of truth and my peace. Don't be afraid.' Only Jesus has lived that fully for all His earthly years, walking 'the Way of Holiness' (see Isaiah 35:8) with integrity to its bitter, then glorious end.

Many now, like Gentiles of Jesus' day, think of truth primarily as intellectual, defending their case by quoting this authority or that. Emotional and spiritual truths are often less clear-cut. Complex problems and questions such as 'What is the right or most loving thing to do in this situation?' aren't easy to answer and seldom did Jesus' words or actions show the kind of truth anyone expected or thought they knew. All becomes clearer by getting to know Christ the Word, rather than by finding biblical texts to support our own religious dogmatism. I'm no longer free to 'do things my way'. Christ's way is expansive, full of love, grace, wonder and humility, rather than rigidity, pride, exclusion or defensiveness. Having Him as Lord can seem uncomfortable and demanding. God will be what He will be. He alone may judge, for He alone sees our inmost thoughts from an immensely wide, eternal perspective, where mercy sits alongside justice and sacrificial love, way above human judgmentalism.

In John 14, Jesus prepares the disciples for His death, and for their lives afterwards. They don't understand. 'Where are you going?' Thomas asks in honest puzzlement. I'm sure most of

'I AM THE WAY, THE TRUTH AND THE LIFE'

us will have asked God: 'What are You doing, Lord? Where are You going with this? How do You want us to act – and when? What good can You possibly redeem from these awful circumstances?' Answers can be slow to arrive and seem as enigmatic as Jesus saying He's going to a house with masses of rooms which He'll prepare for us. Imagine the looks of utter bewilderment! Where was Jesus' huge house and why did He think they knew the way there? I spotted another 'I am' in verse 3, whose literal translation is: 'Again I come and will receive you to myself, that, where am I (*eimi ego*), also you may be.' Is Jesus referring only to life after our bodies' death, or does our eternal life begin from when He renews our relationship with His Father through the cross? Then, having spoken about leaving and going to make a home for them, Jesus turns things around, promising: 'My Father will love them, and we will come to them and make our home with them' (John 14:23). How amazing is that!

When I pray to know the way, often no signposts appear. That's because Jesus *is* the way. He, in turn, does 'only what he sees his Father doing' (John 5:19). By following Him, step by step, in relationship, we'll end up where God wants us. Sheep follow their shepherd's voice without having to see him. Remember, too, Jesus promised the Holy Spirit would 'teach you all things and… remind you of everything I have said to you' (John 14:26), and He would guide us into all truth (16:13).

Notes

Discussion Starters

1. What is the difference between following a set of wise instructions, laws and requirements and following Jesus?

2. How does intellectual understanding of biblical truth differ from getting to know Jesus within a living, loving relationship?

3. Is seeing always believing, or do we have to believe (or at least take a step towards openness and trust) to see the truth and the way?

4. Why does no one come to God as Father except through the way, truth and life of Jesus, His Son?

'I AM THE WAY, THE TRUTH AND THE LIFE'

5. What or who might prevent us following Jesus' way, embracing His truth and receiving His life?

6. What or who might help?

7. How can we embody Jesus' truth, live his 'life in all its fullness' here on Earth and so bring Him glory?

8. From John 14:22–23 it seems Jesus is telling His followers to take on the task of showing others the truth of who the Father is, pointing the way to Him and to the fullness of eternal life. How does Jesus say we are equipped to do this?

Personal Application

Jesus implies that He, the Father and Holy Spirit want to make their home in us. Do we cooperate with them so that they feel increasingly at home in our lives and comfortable with our words, attitudes and activities? Surely we'd do that for honoured human guests? In the 'Opening our Eyes' section you'll find a condensed version of some of Jesus' instructions from John 14. Consider how you might adjust your ways and perception of truth to God's — and where you struggle most to live according to Jesus' way and truth. Ask Him for help to change, from the inside out.

Seeing Jesus in the Scriptures

John 13 describes Jesus eating His last supper with the disciples, knowing one of them will betray Him and one deny Him three times. Very soon He will endure slander, injustice, torture, death and even separation from His beloved Father. But before His arrest (John 18), Jesus spends considerable time teaching, comforting and praying for His disciples (John 15–17). What do you see in Him here? I see extraordinary patience, courage, care and love for His followers at what must have been an agonising time for Him. Jesus' way, truth and life certainly present us with huge challenges. Remember, He also wants us to follow Him by serving others as light, bread, shepherd and all the rest! But alongside His challenges always come His help, support and resources.

WEEK SEVEN
'I AM the Vine; You are the Branches'

Warm Up

Have any of you grown a vine – or any plant with branches that bears fruit, including non-edibles and seeds? Have you learnt anything from it, or maybe God has shown you something through it?

Bible Readings

- John 15:1–17
- Isaiah 5:1–10

Opening our Eyes

The last of the seven 'I ams' in John's Gospel comes within a relatively short but amazing passage. Jesus declared, 'I am the vine' shortly before leaving His disciples to face crucifixion. Having followed Him as the Way, after His death the disciples wait – immobilised, grief-stricken, wilting and vulnerable. Stripped right back, with all hope, faith and trust gone, they have yet to be rooted firmly in Jesus. Later, following Jesus' resurrection and ascension, how remarkably their lives change and what fruit they will bear!

'Abiding' is key here – not a word we use much, except in 'law-abiding' or 'I can't abide something'. The English word abode (where you live) comes from the verb 'to abide' and means more than the NIV's translation: 'remain'. *The Message* uses 'live in', 'make your home in' and 'be joined to'. You might say Jesus' love becomes our lifeblood and our natural habitat. We live in Him and He in us. Whether we're on the road, in our work, in church or enduring difficult times, He's with us, inextricably. Christ makes us part of His vine, at one with Him, as He is with the Father and Holy Spirit, knitted together and empowered by love! Christian faith is not simply belief but an amazingly real relationship with our invisible God that's hard to understand without experiencing it. Paul used the image of us being grafted onto God's vine. He also represented individuals as different functional parts of a human body whose head is Christ. What words or picture-language might you use to express how the relationship between you and Jesus works?

Vineyards appear throughout the Bible. Those prospecting the land God had promised His people returned with a huge bunch of grapes, indicating bountiful fruitfulness (Numbers 13:23). Isaiah 5 and Hosea 2 among others portray Israel as God's vineyard, yet often they rejected His way. Severe 'pruning' might 'lure' them back to Him, restoring fruitfulness, briefly. Finally, God sent His Son as the only Saviour, come to reveal

'I AM THE VINE; YOU ARE THE BRANCHES'

God's exact likeness and truly global intentions. Under the new covenant, Jews persisting in rejecting Jesus cut themselves off from God's vine, while Gentiles loving and believing in Him are grafted into it. (You might look at Jesus' vineyard parables in Matthew chapters 21, 22 and Luke 13. References to us bearing fruit include Galatians 5:22–23, Colossians 1:6 and 9–11.)

We planted two grapevines which grew at an alarming rate over a pergola in our garden, giving us welcome shade. Each autumn, multitudes of tiny grapes appeared; inedible, they produced disgusting wine, while vineyards nearby produced award-winning vintages. They pruned vigorously: we wouldn't hack at our beautiful vines. Most people also hate being cut back or 'pruned', even for our own good. Left to ourselves, we would grow out of control, huge, proud and useless. Then worry, loss, need or suffering act as pruning shears, impelling us to ask God for help. He can turn around woes for our good and that of others, shaping us to be more like Him as we ask for and receive His resources. Perhaps we'll grow in compassion, trust Him more, or learn to be still and wait, secure in His deep-rooted love. Only abiding in that love enables us to obey His seemingly impossible commands to love Him unreservedly and to love others as we do ourselves. It's that nourishing love-sap, those roots holding us secure, that grow good fruit in us.

Notes

 **Discussion Starters**

1. How have you been 'pruned' — by Jesus' words, the Holy Spirit, friends, work, life…?

2. What were the pruning's long-term effects?

3. Does God ever appear to have 'gone away for the winter' while your 'fruit withers'?

4. Do you know how to be still, waiting on God, understanding that, apart from Him, you can do nothing? Or do you always want to push ahead, working things out for yourself?

'I AM THE VINE; YOU ARE THE BRANCHES'

5. Might the branch references (vv5–7) apply corporately – as in branches/groups of a church, bank, or nation? What 'branch/es' are you on? Who 'branches' off you?

6. Jesus' 'root command' is: 'Love one another the way I loved you' (v12). How is that even possible, given the extraordinary extent and purity of Christ's love for us?

7. Of Jesus' 'I am' sayings – light of the world, bread of life, good shepherd, entrance to the sheepfold, way, truth, resurrection, life and true vine – which have you found most helpful and which most challenging?

8. Thinking about applying to your life all God has highlighted for you during these studies, where does each individual need most support from Jesus – and from the group?

Personal Application

How has this whole study changed the way you see Jesus and therefore the way you think, react, act, pray and follow Him? If we are part of His vine, we are part of Him, growing and producing fruit like Him. We'll get nowhere unless we 'abide' secure in His love and feed on Him continually. What changes might you need to make in your daily life in order to do that?

Now consider how you can feed others with His bread, bring them light, be their shepherd-guide, show His way and truth and demonstrate His resurrection life at work in you. How, through your words and actions, can you show how it's possible to be 'at one' in relationship with God through Jesus' work of 'at-one-ment' on the cross, when he defeated the powers of sin and death, opening the gate to eternal life?

Seeing Jesus in the Scriptures

Why not read the rest of John's Gospel, noting all the themes we've considered already. We've missed John 1–5, 7, 9, 12 and 13. Also, most of John 15:18 to the Gospel's end, where Jesus continues to prepare His disciples for what is about to happen, prays for them and for Himself, is arrested, crucified and then raised from the dead. How has considering who Jesus is and how He lived on Earth affected your own sense of identity and the way you live?

Leader's Notes

WEEK ONE: His Name is... 'I AM'

Introduction and 'Opening Our Eyes'
Note that I have over-simplified the derivation of *Yahweh*, which is a primitive form of the first person of the Hebrew verb 'To be'. God says to Moses: *Hayah ash-er hayah*, with both letters 'a' in *hayah* pronounced as in the English word *saw* – so, *Hawyaw*.

Surprisingly, water is not one of the seven 'I ams', despite often representing the divine in Scripture and especially John's Gospel. Jesus promises to give 'living water' in Chapter 4 and, uniquely in John, water as well as blood flow from Jesus' side. Perhaps the water He gives is the Holy Spirit?

Discussion Starters
1. The context appears to stress the eternal nature of God but I wonder if 'That I am' might imply more, such as: all-sufficient, beyond human understanding, no explanation required, sovereign, uniquely God.

2. Steer away from attempts to unravel the mystery of three Persons in one God!

5. From John 1 we learn that the Word (as John calls the pre-incarnate Jesus) was eternal (with God from the beginning), creating 'everything that was made'. In Him was life (one of John's other main themes is eternal life) and 'the light of all mankind', mightier than any darkness. He gives those who receive and believe in Him the right to become God's children. Jesus, who is at one with His Father God, has come to literally 'pitch His tent' among us. Despite the mess we made of God's creation, He lived here full of glory, grace and truth, fully God and fully man. All of that is in the Prologue!

6. After the Prologue, we learn that the way is being made straight for Him in the wilderness, as was prophesied in Isaiah 40:3, and that He is the Lamb of God. Remember, John the Baptist did not know Jesus was to die at the Jewish festival of Passover. That's when each family would kill a lamb to remember when God freed them from slavery in Egypt. (He'd told them to daub their doorways with its blood so their firstborn would be spared death.) Jesus is God's Chosen One who will 'baptise with the Holy Spirit' ('baptise' means 'immerse'). He is also called Rabbi (a Jewish teacher) and the Anointed One (Messiah or Christ in Greek).

7. Joseph's son from the unimportant village of Nazareth is revealed as the Son of God, King of Israel, and the Son of Man, come to make His Father known, so we can be saved and become God's children too. All this conveyed in one chapter, astounding! Angels ascending and descending refers to Genesis 28:12 ('Jacob's ladder'). 'Son of Man' was a phrase often used simply to mean a human person but Daniel 7:13–14 says: 'In my vision at night I looked, and there before me was one like a son of man, coming with the clouds of heaven. He approached the Ancient of Days and was led into his presence. He was given authority, glory and sovereign power; all nations and peoples of every language worshipped him. His dominion is an everlasting dominion that will not pass away, and his kingdom is one that will never be destroyed.' Jewish thinking

LEADER'S NOTES

tended to associate the 'Son of Man' with the End Times. Jesus ushered in a new era through His incarnation, death and resurrection and will do so again. According to Mark 14:61–62, when the High Priest asks: 'Are you the Messiah, the Son of the Blessed One?' Jesus says, 'I am. And you will see the Son of Man sitting at the right hand of the Mighty One and coming on the clouds of heaven.'

WEEK TWO: 'I AM the Bread of Life'

General
Concentrate on John 6 but aim to whet appetites. Explore links within John's Gospel and to other parts of the Bible. Jesus' words in John 6 challenge and confront but are not meant to discourage or condemn. Emphasise Jesus' love, forgiveness and restoration whenever we fail Him and then turn back towards Him again.

Warm Up
First check hand hygiene and any allergy issues and remind people that we're looking at 'I am the bread of life' this week. The warm up provides a useful start for this session by demonstrating our multi-layered sharing together. As communion with a small 'c', it may also call to mind how, through the sensory act of eating bread, we remember Jesus' understanding of and care for our bodies as well as our spirits.

Discussion Starters
1. You might draw out how God told Israel to bake bread hastily and to roast lambs as part of their final meal before the angel of death struck down Egypt's firstborn, so initiating the nation's deliverance from slavery. The lambs' blood smeared on Israel's doorposts warned death's angel to 'pass over' (spare) their households. Later, lamb (and bread) become part of the annual Passover meal celebrating God's formative salvation of their nation. Lamb's blood symbolised freedom and life replacing

slavery and death and of course, Christians believe Jesus is the sacrificial Lamb of God. After escaping Egypt, Israel wandered for 40 years around the desert, where God provided ample manna (a bread-like staple) to nourish them all each day. If they tried to hoard the manna overnight, though, it would go bad.

4. 'Unless you eat the flesh of the Son of Man and drink his blood, you have no life in you.' Jesus' words in John 6:53 look like a PR disaster. Consuming any creature's blood, let alone that of a man, was forbidden under *Yahweh's* law and therefore horrific to Jews, who believed the life of a creature resided in its blood. No wonder Jesus lost many 'camp followers' that day – and maybe He needed to! Many were following Him for the wrong reasons, pressing in on Him too much, failing to understand His mission, expecting constant miracles, or that He would overthrow the Romans and become their earthly king. As it was, Jesus alienated many, provoking violent opposition. Early Christians who 'broke bread' together to remember His death were accused of cannibalism and lynched for it. What can we followers of Jesus learn from all this today as we talk with those who don't know Him or don't know Him well? We know Jesus' shocking declarations weren't some terrible mistake – so it's worth considering if we err sometimes by portraying Him as too gentle, meek and mild and the Christian life too easy, too nice, too sanitised. Jesus knew when to be radical and when to hold back and be compassionate – but many of us may well struggle to discern the right balance.

7. See John 6:70–71 and 13:18–30. Might Paul's words in 1 Corinthians 11:23–34 help? Judas' betrayal famously ended with his suicide (a dramatic example of the law of sin and death at work). Yet Paul says in verse 32 that God may discipline but won't condemn us, even if we fail to 'discern the Lord's body' at Communion. The law of life eternal is made possible only by Jesus' self-sacrificial death.

LEADER'S NOTES

WEEK THREE: 'I AM the Light of the World'

General
Concentrate on John 9. In John's Gospel, Jesus enlightens a darkened world – a great image. But God made, and inhabits, darkness as well as light (Isa. 45:7; Exod. 20:21, et al) and darkness doesn't always lead to evil, ignorance, defeat or misery. Acknowledging our own darkness and need makes us receptive to Jesus' light and love. By contrast, the superior attitude of 'law-abiding' Pharisees meant they rejected Jesus and taught that God was punishing blind and disabled people for their sins. Even now, some Christians believe that sin causes physical traits (including darkness of skin) and that these traits denote inferiority! The truth is that we are all sinners – and all equal in God's sight. Only He may judge and only His grace can save.

It's important to follow Jesus' teaching rather than paths leading deeper into selfishness, falsehood and immorality. However, He may well call us to go and shine His light in places made dark by sin. It's also important to remember that we all go through dark, difficult seasons. Jesus, who Himself experienced real darkness, stays with us there (Ps. 23:4; Ps. 139:11–12), guiding perhaps to 'treasures of darkness' (Isa. 45:3, NKJV) and then to bright fields beyond.

Discussion Starters
2. In John 1:5, the word often translated as 'overcome' or 'understood' is the past active of the verb *katalambano*, meaning to take hold of or to seize a territory in war – or to discover or understand something. Appearing 13 times in the New Testament, sometimes it applies to a demon 'seizing' someone, or to receive, perceive, apprehend or comprehend (see John 8:3–4, 12:35; 1 Cor. 9:24; Phil. 3:12–13). The closest English word is 'apprehend' – to perceive, grasp or arrest. *Katalambano* is a strong, active verb. God's light will win; our part is to perceive, to lay hold of and stay with that light.

3. John 8:12 gives a different angle. Perhaps leave people with that assurance at the end of your session.

4. As 'fountain' of our daily lives, the Lord sustains, refreshes and cleanses – and teaches us to see the world, not through rose- or mud-tinted glasses, but through His loving, compassionate, empowering eyes.

5. The Gospels show how religious people, in attempting to 'defend God' from evil and darkness, may become rigidly judgmental and unloving towards their fellow humans. Jesus' fundamental instructions are 'simply' to love the Lord your God with all your heart, soul, mind and strength and love your neighbour as yourself (Mark 12:30–31). Given that love, complex questions of morality, faith and understanding often resolve. Without it, we Christians will have blind spots. 1 John 2:9–10 equates blindness and walking in darkness with lack of love. I've been a Christian for decades, yet God is still working on areas of Pharisee-like blindness in me. He doesn't give up – John himself demonstrates that. At first, Jesus called him and his brother James 'Sons of Thunder' (Mark 3:17), making those fishermen-brothers sound like real 'toughies'. Yet John became Jesus' 'beloved disciple', majoring on love in the letters He wrote later.

6. There's a saying: 'None are so blind as they who will not see'. John highlights the irony of 'enlightened' religious leaders railing against Jesus' kindness in healing the blind man. If you have a copy of C.S. Lewis' *The Last Battle*, do read the last few pages of chapter 13 which contrast the dwarf's view of the stable with that of the children.

8. Matthew 5:14–16 is another example of 'I am, now you are.'

LEADER'S NOTES

WEEK FOUR: 'I AM the Good Shepherd and Gate for the Sheep'

Warm Up

For the brainstorming version, have everyone call out ideas. Don't look them all up or spend time on them. For the active version, again have a five-minute limit, maximum, and don't appoint yourself 'shepherd'.

Discussion Starters

1. There's no one answer since we're all different, but try to draw out different things that people find helpful – for example, spending time with Him, getting to know His voice, listening out for it in Scripture, in songs, in what we see, in words others speak to us. Do we trust Him to guide us when we are uncertain and to shut those gateways we're not to enter? Do we review our day with Him, asking where we've met with and heard Him and where we've followed the wrong lead or our own way – and asking for His forgiveness, help and reshaping?

5. 'Sheep not of this fold' probably refers to Gentiles since Jesus was speaking within His own Jewish nation. We see flocks scattered throughout history; we see splits and schisms. Many Christian groups go astray. But it's remarkable that the light of Christ is still burning, often brightest where there's persecution. No one grouping is perfect. Sometimes we have to agree to disagree, while maintaining respect, love and fellowship as a priority. Sometimes Christ leads us on different routes, at least for a while. Maybe it's time for a once-important group or activity to end well, leaving room for new beginnings. Be sensitive if there is conflict or division within your church or locality. If appropriate, draw out how people are feeling and who might be hurting. Ultimately, we have to depend on Jesus to shepherd us through storms and rocky places. His love and ours eases the way.

6. When Jesus became angry it was almost always at religious leaders exploiting and leading people astray. They judged themselves as superior and others often more by outward appearance than by the heart, the spirit and the fruits. Abuse within churches isn't exclusively sexual or financial. Teaching distortions of God's truth, manipulating people's lives in order to build a leader's own powerbase, laying burdens of guilt on those who have repented, making certain decisions 'unforgiveable', failing to care for the poor, needy and marginalised – all are false shepherding and forms of spiritual abuse.

7. Do look at Matthew 7:13–14.

8. 'I and the Father are one,' (v30). (Jesus could have put it: 'I am one with the Father and the Father is one with me'. And 'I am God's Son'.) Note that, after Jesus died and rose again, the Father gave Him 'all authority in heaven and earth' and it is through that authority he gave us all the Great Commission, promising to be with us always (Matt. 28:18–20). Another passage that may help is Romans 14. We should not judge those who do things a different way or impose our own way upon them. Instead, 'every knee will bow' before God and before Jesus. They have the ultimate authority to direct and to judge: humans who abuse their delegated authority will fall under their judgment. Jesus' words could not be stronger: 'If anyone causes one of these little ones – those who believe in me – to stumble, it would be better for them if a large millstone were hung round their neck and they were thrown into the sea' (Mark 9:42).

WEEK FIVE: 'I AM the Resurrection and the Life'

General
Please note that having looked at 'the life' alongside 'the resurrection' in this current study, we shall concentrate on 'the

LEADER'S NOTES

way and the truth' in the next one. You may find more than enough to explore around the themes of resurrection and life without reading John 20 and 21 and tackling Discussion Starters 6–8. Or you could take a second week to look at those.

Discussion Starters

1. 'Let us also go, that we may die with him' (v16). Because he says these words, I've heard Thomas characterised as a man of gloom and disbelief rather than of faith and power. I disagree: Thomas knew how dangerous it was for Jesus and the disciples to approach Jerusalem at that time. Unlike us, he didn't understand how the story would end yet was still willing to lay down his life for Jesus because he loved and believed in Him (see Jesus' teaching in John 12:25–26).

2. Facing similar dangers previously, Jesus would disappear. Whether He melted into the crowd through human skill or through God's supernatural protection isn't clear. After raising Lazarus, though, knowing that it was very nearly but not quite 'His time', Jesus deliberately withdrew to Ephraim with his close disciples (John 11:54). After that, and one more day in Bethany, He made His 'triumphal entry' into Jerusalem. When Passover crowds cheered Him on, a murderous backlash followed. How do people in your group discern whether or not it's God who is asking them to do something that's risky, for themselves, their family or their fellow Christians?

3. How does the Spirit of Christ give His eternal life to these mortal bodies? (That is, bodies which will deteriorate and die.) Consider Romans 8:11 if you can.

4. Glory is another of John's main themes. He gives less detail than other Gospels about the events leading up to Jesus' death. For example, he omits Jesus' prayer-battle in Gethsemane, except perhaps for something in John 12:27–29 that ends with a voice thundering from heaven in response to Jesus asking His Father to glorify His name: 'I have glorified it, and will glorify it again'. Paradoxically, Jesus being 'lifted up' as a disgraced criminal leads to glorification. The very worst imaginable transforms into the best outcome. Empty cross and empty tomb become symbols of beauty arising from ashes – of powerful new life for billions resulting from one death. How might this affect our responses to shame, disgrace and apparent failure?

5. What does it look like to have the Spirit of Him who raised Jesus from the dead living in and empowering us? Where, in your wider community, do you see broken lives transformed or nature that has been damaged by pollution restored, for example? Where might God be wanting to work with you to transform and revive?

6, 7, 8. If anyone can tell us about resurrection power, it's John, so why not take an extra session on his lengthy final two chapters? The 'beloved disciple', who claims to have been the writer of this Gospel, was also the second to witness the miracle of the empty tomb. Close to Jesus throughout His ministry, in His 'inner three', John saw it all, even remaining at the cross until Jesus died. He seemed to know Jesus more deeply and to have been changed by Him more than any of them (see Leader's Notes Week 3, Discussion Starter 5).

WEEK SIX: 'I AM the Way, the Truth and the Life'

Warm Up
Don't spend too long on these questions – they're just to start everyone thinking about how Jesus, *the* way and *the* truth, can transform lives. Perhaps ask each person to pick one to answer.

Bible Readings
Again, concentrate on John 14.

LEADER'S NOTES

Discussion Starters

1,2. These are similar. Choose whichever would work best with your group. It might help to look at the story of the good Samaritan in Luke 10:25–37. Jesus told it in response to the question raised by an expert in Jewish religious law: 'What must I do to inherit eternal life?' Maybe Jesus' way, truth and life can be simplified like this: love authentically and wholeheartedly, love God and love all people. After all, He loves every other person as much as He loves you. Simple to say: hard for us to do, consistently! But try updating His parable for our twenty-first century – if you can't get to church because you see a stranger in deep trouble, isn't it a no-brainer?

3. You may want to refer back to John 9 (Week 3) or to the many who cried out to Jesus to heal their blindness, contrasted with know-it-all religious types whose physical eyes worked yet were blind to who Jesus was and wouldn't ask Him for help. Of course, unlike those early disciples, we can't see Jesus physically. Those yet to have a relationship with Him often struggle to see how one might work. That's where we come in! A stalwart member of my congregation only became a Christian in her 50s after her daughter had started following Jesus. 'I was amazed at the changes I saw in her,' the mother told me.

4. Jesus' words: 'No one comes to the Father except through me' still spark contention and have been used to exclude followers of other religions and belief systems from ever meeting Him. My understanding is that no one can know God as a Father except through Jesus. Indeed, when Jesus addressed God by the familiar name of *Abba* (meaning 'Daddy') Jewish leaders accused Him of blasphemy. The natural world, other truths and religions may contain much that's spiritually helpful, but only putting faith in Jesus, His life, death and resurrection, can restore the broken relationship between us and His Father. Only a parent can adopt people into his family. No longer mere servants, we become sons and daughters and co-heirs with Christ (See Romans 8:15–17 et al.) This question also opens the way to explore further about how salvation works, which may or may not be suitable for your group.

5 and 6. Things like wanting our own way, dogmatism, fear or worry may hinder us. We're helped, for example, by the Holy Spirit 'of truth' (vv16–17), asking in Jesus' name, trust, humility, His peace and even experiencing opposition (as when Satan proved the truth and integrity of Jesus). To love and obey are vital too. So is being clear about whether we see Jesus as with us on our journey or us with Him on His mission. Is He our Lord and agenda-setter or our personal miracle-worker? Psalm 25, especially verses 4–5, might be helpful for Discussion Starter 6.

7 and 8 approach the same territory as 5 and 6 but from a different angle. End by praying through what you've learnt and especially for individuals struggling with specific challenges. Consider advocating ongoing, honest 'spiritual friendships' in twos or threes to pray, encourage, share vulnerabilities and breakthroughs, and lend support, knowing each other inside out.

WEEK SEVEN: 'I AM the Vine; You are the Branches'

I find The Message's translation particularly helpful in John 15.

Warm Up
It might be helpful if someone brings a pot plant to this session.

Discussion Starters
1 and 2. In John 15, Jesus encourages His disciples before He died. He was not leaving them alone. They would remain in Him. He had 'made his dwelling' among them (John 1:14) and now urges, 'make your home in me just as I do in you' (John 15:4, *The Message*). His life-blood feeds life and empowers our growth as naturally and organically as the sap does the

LEADER'S NOTES

vine. Be aware, though, that references to pruning and being 'thrown into the fire and burned' (v6) may terrify anyone already feeling cut off from God. Are they consigned to His rubbish heap through sin or lack of 'fruit'? No! All Christians sin and, like plants, experience unfruitful seasons. Christ, the vine, wouldn't cut part of Himself off for that, nor, as shepherd-pastor, would He ignore lost sheep and runaway sons: He enables forgiveness and re-connection.

3. Like vines, most Christians endure the dark, wintry seasons of apparent nothingness they need before flowering and fruiting again later. That 'dormant period' is vital. Habakkuk 3:17–19 might help currently 'dormant' individuals in the group, while those who are currently blossoming or fruiting might come alongside to comfort and help to literally 'en-courage' them.

4. Most people tend one way or the other, whereas 'abiding' seems to imply both. Scripture shows godly people doing both too. Encourage your active ones to rest in God sometimes and the contemplative ones to ask where God wants them to act.

5. I don't know the answer but suspect it's 'both'. We're often too quick to assume that Scripture applies chiefly to individuals. In 1 Corinthians 3:10–15, Paul writes about building a church – a local 'branch' of the vine. We all know churches that have gone wrong, split or broken up completely. They might have been founded on God-inspired vision and great motives but it's essential for churches to remain centred on Christ's love, in living relationship with, obedience to and dependence on Him, day by day. Take time also to celebrate all the wonderful networks and interconnections within the 'vine', which is Christ – locally as well as globally. For all the malfunctioning churches that hit the news, very many more remain faithfully following Jesus.

6. Consider which 'root command' of Christ governs those effective relationships. See Jesus' two commands in Mark

12:30–31. We'll know perfection in heaven; till then He'll help our love to grow. That we love because Christ first loved us is radical (from the root) and vital (life-giving) for everyone, every word we speak and action we take. His love is to be celebrated and practised.

7 and 8. There has been a lot to think and pray about every week during this series, so your group might want to take an additional week for these last two questions. Give opportunity to pray over any remaining puzzles about who Jesus is and who He wants us to be – and to lay hold of what we've learnt so that our lives bear more fruit for Him. The great thing about group studies is that people can pray for and support one another, helping each other to understand and keep applying all God has been saying. May Jesus encourage you as you do this together with Him.

Daily Guide

This daily guide is designed to help you to engage with the material in the Study Guide in between the sessions. More copies of this daily guide are available to download for free from **wvly.org/c2ccv.**

Day 1	Complete Week 1 in the Study Guide.
Day 2	Read John 1:1–14 again, several times. What is God highlighting for you today?
Day 3	Prayer for the day – base it on Psalm 46, especially verse 10: 'Be still and know that I am God'.
Day 4	Action – look for opportunities today to share your excitement over something you've discovered about Jesus this week.
Day 5	Read John 8:48–58 again and meditate on one thing which God highlights for you there.
Day 6	Prayer for the day: Lord, help me fix my eyes on You as 'I am' – present, powerful and loving, no matter where I am or what my circumstances are.
Day 7	Action – ask Jesus to help you grasp the implications of 'because He is, we can be' – and so banish some of your fears and self-imposed limitations.
Day 8	Complete Week 2 in the Study Guide.
Day 9	Read Isaiah 55.

Day 10	Prayer for the day: Thank you, Lord, that You came at great cost yet are freely available; please help me 'buy into' and 'consume' You, rather than what society urges.
Day 11	Action – look for opportunities to explain how and why Jesus is even more vital for your growth and sustenance than any staple food.
Day 12	Read John 6 again.
Day 13	Pray for the physically and spiritually hungry.
Day 14	Action – look for opportunities to invite someone in need for a meal.
Day 15	Complete Week 3 in the Study Guide.
Day 16	Read any of the Bible passages listed at the start of this week that you've not had time to read in your group.
Day 17	Pray using these words from 'Hark, the herald angels sing' by Charles Wesley to praise Jesus, 'Light of the world': 'Hail the heaven-born Prince of Peace! Hail the Sun of Righteousness! Light and life to all He brings, risen with healing in His wings.'
Day 18	Action – note down anything that God is highlighting to you from this week's study.
Day 19	Read and meditate on Psalm 36:9.
Day 20	Pray, asking Jesus to alert you to remain in His light and to help you see with His eyes in any areas where you've been blind.
Day 21	Action – lighten someone's darkness by showing them God's love.
Day 22	Complete Week 4 in the Study Guide.
Day 23	Read Luke 15:1–7.
Day 24	Prayer for the day: Help me to hear and respond to Your voice, Lord.
Day 25	Action – look for opportunities to thank someone who leads (or has led) you to follow Jesus more closely.
Day 26	Read Ezekiel 34 and pray about any issues it raises in today's world.

DAILY GUIDE

Day 27	Pray for the leaders of your church and for those in your group who exercise leadership within their family, workplace or neighbourhood.
Day 28	Action – look for opportunities to seek out and care for one of Jesus' sheep who seems a bit lost.
Day 29	Complete Week 5 in the Study Guide.
Day 30	Read John 5:21 and 24–29.
Day 31	Prayer for the day: Lord of life and death, thank you for helping me understand more of the depth and reality of all You did to restore eternal life to us.
Day 32	Action – spend time with Jesus, as though you were a close friend, walking with Him through all that happened in this week's readings.
Day 33	Read and meditate on John 12:24–26.
Day 34	Prayer for the day: Lord, help me to lay down my possessions, my rights or even my life if You ask me to – and to keep my hope and trust in You.
Day 35	Action – Look for opportunities to comfort and give hope to someone who mourns, or who fears dying.
Day 36	Complete Week 6 in the Study Guide.
Day 37	Read again any one of this week's four passages, or read any that you missed.
Day 38	Prayer for the day: Lord, Your way and Your truth can seem so counterintuitive sometimes; thank You for Your grace, kindness and patience when we misunderstand.
Day 39	Action – ask the Holy Spirit to work with you on a spiritual audit of your life.
Day 40	Read John 13 or Psalm 25.
Day 41	Pray for anyone you know who has gone after a false truth or is following a dangerous way.
Day 42	Action – come alongside someone you prayed for yesterday, guiding them with patience, grace and love towards Jesus.
Day 43	Complete Week 7 in the Study Guide.

The Cover to Cover Bible Study Series

CHARACTERS

Abraham
Adventures of faith
ISBN: 978-1-78259-089-7

Barnabas
Son of encouragement
ISBN: 978-1-85345-911-5

David
A man after God's own heart
ISBN: 978-1-78259-444-4

Elijah
A man and his God
ISBN: 978-1-85345-575-9

Elisha
A lesson in faithfulness
ISBN: 978-1-78259-494-9

Jacob
Taking hold of God's blessing
ISBN: 978-1-78259-685-1

Joseph
The power of forgiveness and reconciliation
ISBN: 978-1-85345-252-9

Mary
The mother of Jesus
ISBN: 978-1-78259-402-4

Moses
Face to face with God
ISBN: 978-1-85345-336-6

THEMES

Bible Genres
Hearing what the Bible really says
ISBN: 978-1-85345-987-0

Covenants
God's promises and their relevance today
ISBN: 978-1-85345-255-0

The Creed
Belief in action
ISBN: 978-1-78259-202-0

The Divine Blueprint
God's extraordinary power in ordinary lives
ISBN: 978-1-85345-292-5

Fruit of the Spirit
Growing more like Jesus
ISBN: 978-1-78951-495-7

God's Rescue Plan
Finding God's fingerprints on human history
ISBN: 978-1-85345-294-9

Great Prayers of the Bible
Applying them to our lives today
ISBN: 978-1-85345-253-6

The Holy Spirit
Understanding and experiencing Him
ISBN: 978-1-85345-254-3

NEW: I Ams
Who is Jesus?
ISBN: 978-1-78951-499-5

The Image of God
His attributes and character
ISBN: 978-1-85345-228-4

Names of God
Exploring the depths of God's character
ISBN: 978-1-85345-680-0

NEW: Revive Your Church
Seeking and encountering abundant life
ISBN: 978-1-78951-441-4

Rivers of Justice
Responding to God's call to righteousness today
ISBN: 978-1-85345-339-7

The Second Coming
Living in the light of Jesus' return
ISBN: 978-1-85345-422-6

The Uniqueness of our Faith
What makes Christianity distinctive?
ISBN: 978-1-85345-232-1

NEW: Violence against Women
Discovering El Roi, The God Who Sees
ISBN: 978-1-78951-445-2

NEW TESTAMENT

NEW: Matthew
Your Kingdom Come
ISBN: 978-1-78951-450-6

Mark
Life as it is meant to be lived
ISBN: 978-1-85345-233-8

Luke
A prescription for living
ISBN: 978-1-78259-270-9

John's Gospel
Exploring the seven miraculous signs
ISBN: 978-1-85345-295-6

Acts 1–12
Church on the move
ISBN: 978-1-85345-574-2

Acts 13–28
To the ends of the earth
ISBN: 978-1-85345-592-6

The Letter to the Romans
Good news for everyone
ISBN: 978-1-85345-250-5

1 Corinthians
Growing a Spirit-filled church
ISBN: 978-1-78951-510-7

2 Corinthians
Restoring harmony
ISBN: 978-1-85345-551-3

Galatians
Freedom in Christ
ISBN: 978-1-85345-648-0

Ephesians
Claiming your inheritance
ISBN: 978-1-85345-229-1

Philippians
Living for the sake
of the gospel
ISBN: 978-1-85345-421-9

The Letter to the Colossians
In Christ alone
ISBN: 978-1-855345-405-9

Thessalonians
Building Church in
changing times
ISBN: 978-1-78259-443-7

1 Timothy
Healthy churches –
effective Christians
ISBN: 978-1-85345-291-8

2 Timothy and Titus
Vital Christianity
ISBN: 978-1-85345-338-0

Philemon
From slavery to freedom
ISBN: 978-1-85345-453-0

Hebrews
Jesus – simply the best
ISBN: 978-1-85345-337-3

James
Faith in action
ISBN: 978-1-85345-293-2

1 Peter
Good reasons for hope
ISBN: 978-1-78259-088-0

2 Peter
Living in the light of
God's promises
ISBN: 978-1-78259-403-1

1,2,3 John
Walking in the truth
ISBN: 978-1-78951-501-5

Revelation 1–3
Christ's call to the Church
ISBN: 978-1-85345-461-5

Revelation 4–22
The Lamb wins! Christ's
final victory
ISBN: 978-1-85345-411-0

The Armour of God
Living in His strength
ISBN: 978-1-78259-583-0

The Beatitudes
Immersed in the grace of Christ
ISBN: 978-1-78259-495-6

The Lord's Prayer
Praying Jesus' way
ISBN: 978-1-85345-460-8

Parables
Communicating God on earth
ISBN: 978-1-85345-340-3

Prayers of Jesus
Hearing His heartbeat
ISBN: 978-1-85345-647-3

The Prodigal Son
Amazing grace
ISBN: 978-1-85345-412-7

The Sermon on the Mount
Life within the new covenant
ISBN: 978-1-85345-370-0

OLD TESTAMENT

Genesis 1–11
Foundations of reality
ISBN: 978-1-85345-404-2

Genesis 12–50
Founding fathers of faith
ISBN: 978-1-78259-960-9

Exodus
God's Epic Rescue
ISBN: 978-1-78951-272-4

The Ten Commandments
Living God's Way
ISBN: 978-1-85345-593-3

Joshua 1–10
Hand in hand with God
ISBN: 978-1-85345-542-7

Joshua 11–24
Called to service
ISBN: 978-1-78951-138-3

Judges 1–8
The spiral of faith
ISBN: 978-1-85345-681-7

Judges 9–21
Learning to live God's way
ISBN: 978-1-85345-910-8

Ruth
Loving kindness in action
ISBN: 978-1-85345-231-4

Nehemiah
Principles for life
ISBN: 978-1-85345-335-9

Esther
For such a time as this
ISBN: 978-1-85345-511-7

Job
The source of wisdom
ISBN: 978-1-78259-992-0

Psalms
Songs of life
ISBN: 978-1-78951-240-3

23rd Psalm
The Lord is my shepherd
ISBN: 978-1-85345-449-3

Proverbs
Living a life of wisdom
ISBN: 978-1-85345-373-1

Ecclesiastes
Hard questions and
spiritual answers
ISBN: 978-1-78951-508-4

Song of Songs
A celebration of love
ISBN: 978-1-78259-959-3

Isaiah 1–39
Prophet to the nations
ISBN: 978-1-85345-510-0

Isaiah 40–66
Prophet of restoration
ISBN: 978-1-85345-550-6

Jeremiah
The passionate prophet
ISBN: 978-1-85345-372-4

Ezekiel
A prophet for all times
ISBN: 978-1-78259-836-7

Daniel
Living boldly for God
ISBN: 978-1-78951-503-9

Hosea
The love that never fails
ISBN: 978-1-85345-290-1

Joel
Getting real with God
ISBN: 978-1-78951-927-2

Jonah
Rescued from the depths
ISBN: 978-1-78259-762-9

Habakkuk
Choosing God's way
ISBN: 978-1-78259-843-5

Haggai
Motivating God's people
ISBN: 978-1-78259-686-8

Zechariah
Seeing God's bigger picture
ISBN: 978-1-78951-263-2

For current prices or to order, visit **waverleyabbeytrust.org/publishing**